THE SPITTING COBRAS
OF AFRICA

by James Martin

Illustrated with photographs

by Joe McDonald

Reading consultant:

John Manning, Professor of Reading, University of Minnesota

Capstone Press
MINNEAPOLIS

Printed in the United States of America.

Capstone Press • 2440 Fernbrook Lane • Minneapolis, MN 55447

Editorial Director   John Coughlan
Managing Editor   John Martin
Copy Editor   Gil Chandler

Library of Congress Cataloging-in-Publication Data

Martin, James, 1950-
    The spitting cobras of Africa / by James Martin.
        p. cm.
    Includes bibliographical references and index.
    ISBN 1-56065-239-X
    1. Spitting Cobras--Africa--Juvenile literature.
[1. Cobras. 2. Poisonous snakes. 3. Snakes.]   I. Title.
QL666.O64M37   1995
597.96--dc20   94-30268
                                                CIP
                                                AC

ISBN: 1-56065-239-X

99 98 97 96 95   8 7 6 5 4 3 2 1

Table of Contents

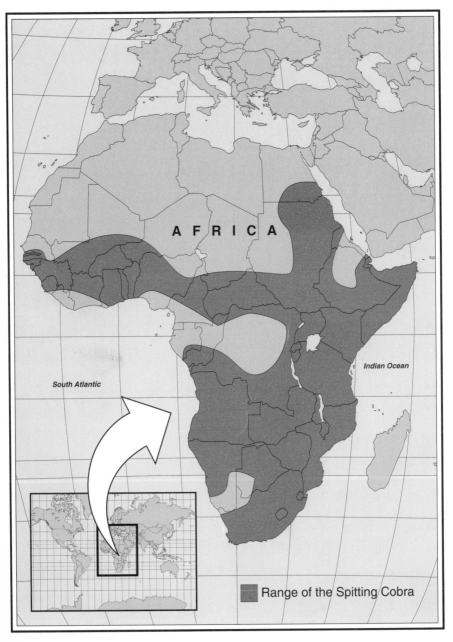

A F R I C A

South Atlantic

Indian Ocean

Range of the Spitting Cobra

Facts about Spitting Cobras

Scientific names: *Hemachatus haemachatus* (the ringhal), *Naja nigricollis* (the black-necked cobra), and *Naja mossambica pallida* (the Mozambique spitting cobra or red spitter).

Description:

Length: Adults are an average of 5 feet (1.5 meters). They have been known to grow as long as 9 feet (2.7 meters).

Physical features: The spitting cobra is sleek. A hood on its head makes it appear larger to enemies.

Color: Ringhals are black with white markings. Black-necked cobras range from pure black to brick-red with black stripes.

Distinctive habits: Spitting cobras spray poison from their fangs. The poison is harmless unless it lands in an eye or a cut.

Food: Rodents, birds, eggs, and reptiles. Some ringhals eat only toads.

Reproduction: Cobras lay eggs in holes and leave them. The babies must care for themselves after hatching.

Life span: Cobras live up to 22 years in captivity.

Range: The black-necked cobra lives in Kenya, Tanzania, and Senegal. Ringhals live in South Africa.

Habitat: Black-necked cobras live in dry fields and open woodlands. Ringhals prefer desert conditions.

Chapter 1
Spitting Cobras

On the high plains of East Africa, strange towers of red dirt dot the landscape. They look like small skyscrapers. But they are not the work of humans. Thousands of busy termites built these towers. Inside, there is a complicated system of passages and tunnels. The tunnels work like an air conditioner to keep the inside cool and pleasant.

Spitting cobras often live in these mounds.

Cobras

Cobras are **venomous** snakes that live in Africa and Asia, mostly in the hot regions along the earth's **equator**. Over the years, some species of cobras moved from the mainland to islands in the Philippines and Indonesia.

Cobras belong to the **Elapidae**, a group of venomous snakes. While some venomous snakes, like vipers, swing their long **fangs** forward and stab their victims, cobras must use their fangs to bite.

Spitting Cobras

Three kinds of cobras, however, prefer spitting to biting: the ringhal (*Hemachatus haemachatus*) and the black-necked cobra (*Naja nigricollis*) of southern Africa and the Mozambique spitting cobra, or red spitter (*Naja mossambica pallida*), of east Africa.

Spitting cobras prefer to live in the hot regions along the earth's equator.

When they bite, spitting cobras actually spray venom out of their fangs.

Striking

Venomous snakes strike in different ways. Vipers and pit vipers, like rattlesnakes, coil themselves tightly and strike sideways. They attack quickly and then recoil to prepare for another strike.

Cobras raise their heads high and strike downward. Cobras are slower than vipers. They probably learned to strike with their heads high. This way, they could threaten their target and then attack instantly.

Pretending to be Large

Pretending to be large is a common **bluff** in the animal world. Cobras have an unusual way of doing this. As they raise their heads, they also expand their hoods. The neck muscles in the hood spread a series of small ribs outward.

Cobras raise their heads high and strike downward.

Rattlesnakes coil themselves tightly and strike sideways.

As it waves back and forth, the snake looks much larger than it really is. It's only a threat, but a cobra's threat should be taken seriously.

Fangs

Most poisonous snakes inject their venom from holes in the backs of their fangs. Spitting cobras have the opening of the fang in the front, so they can spray the venom forward.

Spitting

When spitting cobras raise themselves to threaten an enemy, they are getting ready to spray or bite. They prefer to spray. To do this, a snake pulls its head back for a moment and then whips it forward, like a baseball pitcher throwing a pitch. At the same time, venom shoots out of its fangs. The spray can fly 6 to 7 feet (1.8 to 2.1 meters). If the venom touches the eyes, temporary or permanent blindness, as well as intense pain, results.

If the poison misses the eyes or an open wound, it is harmless. A filmmaker in Africa once wanted to record a spitting cobra spraying venom. He persuaded his wife to put on a pair

of glasses and **pester** a spitting cobra. The **enraged** snake sprayed her in the face, but the poison had no effect. The glasses protected her.

Keeping Enemies at a Distance

Spraying poison gives the snake an advantage. It can attack from a distance. If an enemy can't get close, it can't hurt the snake. Some authorities believe that these cobras developed spraying to keep antelope and other hoofed animals from stepping on them.

Spitting cobras use spraying only for defense. When hunting, they bite their prey. Then they hold and swallow the dead or dying animal.

Venom

Cobras and other members of the Elapidae use a **neurotoxin** to disable their prey. These poisons can stop hearts from beating and lungs from breathing. The toxins contain an **enzyme** to move the poison through the body quickly. The strength of the venom varies with individual snakes. A younger and healthier snake carries stronger poison than an old one. Poisonous snakes bite more than one million people every year. About 50,000 bite victims die.

They have no teeth for chewing, only for striking and holding. Their teeth curve backwards so the prey can't escape. Because a cobra's jaw unhinges, the snake can swallow animals bigger than its own head.

Another Defense: Playing Dead

The spitting cobra has many weapons, but it will often play dead rather than fight. It lies on the ground with its mouth open and its tongue hanging out. If a spitting cobra plays dead, most animals will just ignore it.

A spitting cobra rears back and spits a poisonous venom at its target.

Chapter 2
Life as a Cobra

Try to imagine living as a cobra. Since you have no arms or legs, you can't walk or hold anything. It's hard to defend yourself against danger. Your only weapons are the fangs in your head.

You have only one lung. Your heart has three **chambers** (mammal hearts have four). With a single lung, your simple heart cannot transport much oxygen to the muscles. This means you tire quickly. You are **cold-blooded**, so you need the sun to heat your body enough to move and to digest food.

The Egyptian banded cobra

No Eyelids

You can never close your eyes, because you have no eyelids. There is only a thin layer of clear skin that protects the eyes.

This may sound terrible to us, but cobras make good use of their bodies. With no arms or legs, they can move silently and surprise their prey. Their soft, flexible bodies also can squeeze into the small dens of mice and birds. Wherever an animal hides, a cobra can follow.

Cobras can also go for long periods without food. A reptile needs only a tenth of the food a mammal needs. When food is scarce, snakes can survive longer than mammals or birds.

Smelling without a Nose

Cobras have a sharp sense of smell. But they don't have noses. Instead, they smell with their tongues and their mouths. The tongue collects smells and then touches an organ on the roof of the mouth. It is this organ that recognizes the smell.

Forked Tongue

Its forked tongue allows the cobra to find its prey. One fork is always closer to the source of a smell than the other fork. The fork that's closer detects a stronger smell. This tells the snake what direction to go to find the smell.

How Snakes Move

The skin of a cobra is made up of thousands of scales. The scales on the bottom of the snake grow into large plates. These plates help the snake move.

Snakes move in three ways. In the "accordion" method, the snake pushes its body forward from the rear. It stretches out its body, grips the ground with its front, and then pulls up the rear again. The snake looks like an accordion as it stretches and pulls.

Some snakes, like the sidewinder, loop themselves like a **lariat**. They can move

Snakes have different ways of pulling and pushing themselves along the ground. This cobra uses the "caterpillar" method.

quickly without straightening out. Other snakes, like the cobra, use a caterpillar motion. Each section of the snake's underside lifts, holds, and pushes. As the cycle repeats, the snake seems to flow over the ground.

Eating Habits of Cobras

Different spitting cobras have different eating habits. Black-necked cobras hunt from

The savannah monitor likes to sun itself on top of termite mounds. It searches the ground for food. If a cobra emerges from the mound, the monitor pounces.

The monitor probably would win the battle. It would seize the snake with its jaws. It would whip the snake back and forth on the ground.

The monitor lizard has a thin, clear cover over its eyes that protects it from the snake's venom. Even if the snake could sink its fangs into the lizard's back, the monitor would not be harmed. When the snake stops moving, the lizard gulps it down, dead or alive.

An Enemy Mammal

In "Rikki-Tikki-Tavi," a story by Rudyard Kipling, a mongoose fights two cobras. Mongooses are a kind of weasel. They are very fast–faster than cobras. They kill and eat cobras. But spitting cobras don't need to be as fast as other snakes to escape mongooses.

sunset to sunrise. They eat anything they can swallow–frogs, birds, eggs, small mammals, and other snakes. Many ringhals of southern Africa live on a steady diet of toads. The Mozambique spitting cobra sneaks into hen houses to dine on eggs or small chickens.

Eggs and Babies

Female cobras lay about a dozen eggs in the nest. Eight to ten weeks later, the baby snakes emerge. The babies are only ten to twelve inches (.3 meter) long. The young cobras feed on insects until they grow large enough for bigger meals.

Chapter 3

Enemies

The spitting cobra has both animal and human enemies.

The Savannah Monitor

The savannah monitor is the spitting cobra's worst enemy. It is a cousin of the Komodo dragon, the largest living lizard. A savannah monitor wouldn't pass by a cobra that was playing dead. Instead, it would swallow the cobra whole.

The Indian cobra strikes fear into its enemies with its upraised hood.

Chapter 4

Cobras and Other Elapids

Elapids are a group of venomous snakes that includes cobras, coral snakes, sea snakes, mambas, and others. The oldest Elapid fossils are 15 million years old, from the **Miocene Era**. They once lived in Europe, but none now live on that continent.

Australian Elapids

Australia has the greatest number of Elapids. The smallest Australian Elapid is the bandy-bandy. It is only 18 inches (46 centimeters) long and rarely bites. The largest is the ten-foot (3-meter) taipan, an aggressive and very poisonous snake. About one cobra-bite victim in ten dies. But no one can survive a taipan bite.

The only Elapids in North, Central, and South America are the coral snakes. Two beautiful red-and-black-banded species live in Florida and Arizona. There are 48 other species of coral snake that live in Mexico, Central America, and South America. All other poisonous snakes that live in the Americas are vipers.

African Elapids

In Africa, cobras and mambas, both Elapids, live in almost every part of the continent. Tree cobras and several species of mambas hunt high in the branches. Water cobras spend their days hunting in rivers and lakes.

The Egyptian banded cobra

The King Cobra

The king cobra, also known as the *hamadryad*, is the largest poisonous snake in the world. Although its average length is ten feet (3 meters), one specimen of king cobra reached 18 feet (6 meters). The largest ones can rear 4 feet (1.2 meters) in the air.

The king cobra is also known as the snake-eater, which is the translation of its Latin name. These are the only snakes that build nests for their eggs. The female gathers rotting leaves by sweeping along the ground with her body. She deposits up to fifty eggs, then stands guard for two to three months until the eggs hatch.

Sea Snakes

Sea snakes are among the most poisonous snakes in the world. Their venom is several times more deadly than a cobra's. Their skin allows water, but not salt, to pass through.

The king cobra *(right)* is the world's largest poisonous snake.

They also have a special gland to get rid of any salt that collects in their bodies. Most species of sea snake do not lay eggs. Instead, they give birth to live **offspring**.

The African spitting cobra *(above)* and the Indian cobra *(left)* are two common members of the Elapid family.

Chapter 5

A Survival Strategy

The millions of species that live on earth have found many different ways to survive. While hiding, squid become transparent. While hunting, chameleons shoot their tongues out farther than the lengths of their bodies. Peregrine falcons can swoop down on their prey at 200 miles (322 kilometers) per hour.

Spitting cobras have found a very special way to survive. Spitting cobras are the most specialized members of a very specialized group of snakes. Most snakes don't use poison at all. Of those that do, only the spitting cobras spray it. It's a very effective way of saying, "Don't tread on me!"

Glossary

bluff–to fool or trick

chambers–the separate parts of a heart

cold-blooded–having a body temperature that changes with the surroundings

Elapidae–a family of poisonous snakes that includes spitting cobras

enraged–to become extremely angry

enzyme–a substance produced in living plants and animals that works as a helper in the life process of that plant or animal

equator–the imaginary line circling the earth halfway between the North and South Poles

fang–a snake's long, sharp tooth, with either a groove or a hollow space for poison

lariat–a lasso

Miocene Era–an ancient period of time from about 25 million to 15 million years ago

neurotoxin–a poison that attacks the nervous system

offspring–the young that are born to a set of parents

pester–to disturb or annoy

venomous–having a poison gland

To Learn More

Allen, Missy and Michel Peissel. *Dangerous Reptile Creatures.* New York: Chelsea House, 1993.

Fichter, George S. *Poisonous Snakes.* New York: F. Watts, 1982.

Freedman, George S. *Killer Snakes.* New York: Holiday House, 1982.

Green, Carl R. and William R. Sanford. *The Cobra.* Mankato, MN: Crestwood House, 1986.

Johnson, Sylvia A. *Snakes.* Minneapolis: Lerner, 1986.

Simon, Seymour. *Poisonous Snakes.* New York: Four Winds Press, 1981.

Smith, Roland. *Snakes in the Zoo.* Brookfield, CT: Millbrook, 1992.

Kipling, Rudyard. "Rikki-Tikki-Tavi" in *The Jungle Book* (1894).

D'Amato, Janet and Alex D'Amato. *African
Animals Through African Eyes.* New York:
J. Messner, 1971.

Montroll, John. *African Animals in Origami.*
New York: Dover, 1991.

Some Useful Addresses

World Wildlife Fund
1250 24th St. N.W.
Washington, DC 20037

Canadian Wildlife Federation/Federation canadienne de la faune
2740 Queensview Drive
Ottawa ON K2B 1A2

Society for the Study of Amphibians and Reptiles
P.O. Box 626
Hays, KS 67601-0626

Canadian Amphibian and Reptile Conservation Society
9 Mississauga Rd. N., #1
Mississauga ON L5H 2H5

Friends of the Earth
218 D St. S.E.
Washington, DC 20003

Index

Mozambique spitting
   cobra, 5, 8, 25
muscles, 11, 19

Nairobi, Kenya, 31
neurotoxins, 15

peregrine falcons, 41
Philippines, 8
poison, 5, 8, 11, 13,
   15, 29, 41

rattlesnakes, 11
reproduction, 5, 25,
   36, 39
reptiles, 5
ringhal cobras, 5, 8, 25
rodents, 5

salt, 36, 39
savannah monitors, 27,
   29

scales, 23
scientific names, 5
sea snakes, 8, 33, 36,
   39
sidewinder snakes, 23-
   24
skin, 23, 36
smell, 21, 23
squid, 41

taipans, 34
teeth, 17
termites, 7, 29
toads, 5
tongues, 17, 21, 23